Whispers
of
Love

Whispers *of* Love

HIS MERCY ENDURETH FOREVER

❖

Christina Maclean

AMBASSADOR

BELFAST ◆ **GREENVILLE**
NORTHERN IRELAND ◆ SOUTH CAROLINA

Whispers of Love

© Copyright 1997 Christina Maclean

ISBN 1 84030 002 7

AMBASSADOR PRODUCTIONS LTD,
Providence House
16 Hillview Avenue,
Belfast, BT5 6JR
Northern Ireland

Emerald House,
1 Chick Springs Road, Suite 206
Greenville,
South Carolina 29609
United States of America

Preface

--- ❖ ---

This short book is written at the request of some friends as a sequel to my first book, 'To Everything a Purpose'. Composed in the same simple style it relates a fragmented but honest account of God's dealings with me during the past eighteen months. As it goes forth, it is my prayer that God will bless its contents to fellow sufferers and others. This alone will make the effort worthwhile.

The proceeds are to be donated to the local hospice and for this reason I hope it will be supported.

My thanks to Carol Somerville who undertook the typing of the manuscript, to Rev. A.M. Macleod, Dianne Saunders and Isa Arthur who checked chapters 2, 4, 6 and 7 respectively, and to Rev. K.M. Ferguson who wrote the foreword.

Christina Maclean

Foreword

---------------------- ❖ ----------------------

Readers of Miss Maclean's first book "To Everything A Purpose" will be glad to have this her second publication, in which her self disclosure continues; clearly professional and matter of fact yet warm and distinctly Christian.

Her gracious responses to her cancer and its debilitating effects will be a source of encouragement to many cancer victims and others who endure different forms of suffering and pain. There is precious counsel here for many.

The history of the Bethesda Nursing Home and Hospice is delineated and the author, on retiring from her position as Matron/Manager used her time not only to write but to travel, despite pain and discomfort. Clearly, though the flesh be weak, there is much that can be done if the spirit be willing.

A long standing desire to go to Africa was realised when she visited a mission in Guinea Bissau, West Africa. She also travelled to warwounded Croatia. Out of these foreign trips came a clearer realisation of the needs that are prevalent in these lands and in response to these needs being made known, funds were forthcoming in a wonderful way to finance different projects.

Although Miss Maclean does not specify the nature of the Investiture at Buckingham Palace, she was in fact awarded the M.B.E. in November 1996 in recognition of her services to the Hospice movement.

This story is essentially autobiographical. However, it is not so in an exclusive way, because we find ourselves in the company of one who encourages, challenges and edifies. In fact, one who directs us heavenwards and encourages us to place our hope and confidence in God alone.

Rev. K.M. Ferguson
Chairman, Bethesda Management Committee
Bethesda Hospice,
Springfield Road
Stornoway,
Isle of Lewis
HS1 2PS

28th February 1997

Contents

❖

To

W. M. B.

"When at the first I took my
pen in hand Thus for to write, I
did not understand That I at all
should make a little book In such
a mode; nay, I had undertook
To make another; which when
almost done, Before I was
aware I thus begun."

John Bunyan

Chapter One

Loosening The Roots

❖

'The Lord will perfect that which concerneth me'.
Psa. 138:8

"Ninety six titles under the broad heading of bereavement", I said incredulously, to no one in particular. I couldn't believe that one medical bookshop could stock so many. In addition every journal seemed to carry several reviews and advertise a plethora of training packages on bereavement counselling. Why, I thought, had society become so preoccupied with this subject? I had no wish to decry situations where amelioration had come through counselling, but in the context of the millions bereaved every day, the numbers must be very small. The fact that this material appeared to be neither biblically based nor Christ centred was of obvious concern.

I was at this time greatly exercised as to what I should do regarding my employment. I was really happy in my work, but now that I had presented with my fourth bone metastasis, this time in spine, I felt I should give serious thought to the future of the organisation which I headed as Matron/Manager.

Ever since I first developed cancer in 1979 I always said I would leave while I was still well enough to see my successor appointed. I felt it would be wrong to remain in office until I required to be 'carried'. Now I must make this difficult decision. I was remarkably well after my radiotherapy in December 1994 and felt I could maintain the high standards I set myself, but for how long? Selfishly, I also pondered how I could usefully employ my talents if I retired.

As December melted into January 1995 my conviction grew that I should resign. My love for my workplace and the Lord who made it all so possible had to take precedence and so when the Chairman returned in February I handed in my notice. My roots were loosened and I felt at peace. It was October of that year before I finally left.

When my decision became known, concerned friends and colleagues urged me to employ my free time writing. I certainly considered it and gave an undertaking that if I did write another book the proceeds would be donated to the hospice. But what should I write about? Bereavement from a Christian perspective? I certainly had experience in this field, both from a personal and professional viewpoint, but was this enough? My concerns as a Christian roused me from indifference. Why, I thought, was this era more than any other attaching such tremendous importance to observed grief? I found myself examining the comprehensive aims of these well appointed courses and the audiences they targeted and asked myself how their acclaim to success in the handling of sensitive emotional issues could be achieved when the Lord, the consolation of the bereaved, was left out or barely alluded to.

In this maze of bereavement services and learning packages the Christian's supportive role is diminished and the biblical injunction, 'weep with those who weep' in many instances overlooked. The Christian has the most comprehensive package available - the Word of God. His promises opens the door to the management of grief and promotes the necessary emotional healing through the long painful journey of adapting to loss.

Mourning in biblical times was expressed by weeping and loud lamentation. The first instance of elegy is the lamentation of David over Saul and Jonathan. But there was also the wearing of sackcloth, fasting and sitting in silence. Near relatives sat in their homes with their faces covered and ate on the ground. They were unable to apply themselves to their daily work. This period of mourning usually lasted from 30 to 70 days. Perhaps the problems for our generation arise from our departure from this mourning sequence. We consider calmness as an appropriate expression of manly grief and have developed brave stoical attitudes which in many instances are not helpful to us. One thing the Bible clearly shows is that bereavement has a natural outcome.

These thoughts brought with them an urge to write and during January and part of February 1995 I filled four exercise books with jottings and researched thought. In the third week of February an episode of pain set my pen aside and silenced my thoughts on the subject.

In April of the same year I attended a conference lecture in Tarbert, Harris. Suddenly, I found myself praying, 'What will thou have me to do?' I didn't want to spend what was left of my life in useless inactivity. What could be more lamentable than a 'redundant' Christian. I longed to go to Africa. But with my health record what could I do in that country? And then quite unexpectedly I received a request to go to Kenya, was this an answer to prayer? I couldn't turn it down, yet, neither could I go unless I received clear guidance from the Lord. I had no difficulty believing the Lord was able to control every cancer cell and to keep pain in abeyance but still I hesitated. In August I turned the request down, not without regret, I desperately wanted to go, but it was not the Lord's commission.

Shortly after this I felt my roots were being dug up little by little. Writing for longish periods became a problem and I developed a definite stoop. A sense of uselessness prevailed and yet there was submission, a firm belief in God's plan and in His promise not to forsake His child. The believer is not exempt from suffering and affliction and the valley experience can be very real but, 'He compasseth them with His presence', so that the valley becomes the very forecourt of Heaven.

It was about this time I found my thoughts returning to writing. The Lord had previously told me that whatsoever my hands found to do I must do it. I examined what little I had written on the local hospice. It was not enough. In any case, I was concerned that the subject, now largely history, might not sell well enough to pay the publisher's costs. What did the Lord want me to do? Some friends believed I was going to be healed and I would then write on this subject. But I wasn't healed and I required to apply myself now as, humanly speaking, time was not on my side. I returned to my jottings. Should I write on death and bereavement? I allowed my thoughts to wander. There was young Coinneach, only four years of age, but already experiencing the sheer despair of lost love. "Where's my dad?", was his first question on discovering the empty bed. His dad was sick when he left but he had raised himself up and kissed him, now the room was strangely quiet and his search brought nothing forth. Had he known the words of Milton and been able to comprehend them they would have expressed his feelings accurately.

'But Oh! the heavy change now thou art gone,
Now thou art gone and never must return'.

That his father was in Heaven with Jesus brought no relief to Coinneach. He went outside only to return and defiantly announce, "I met Jesus out there and I punched Him", not a tear, just sheer frustration and anger. The angel of death rends the heart of the child as it does the heart of the adult. Would counselling have helped? Not unless the counsellor knew the power of the Cross, central to effective counselling, and the Lord's endearment towards children, as found in His words, 'Suffer little children to come unto me and forbid them not'. Fulness of grace, comfort, hope, succour and every other blessing is available in Christ. Millions in Glory were succoured during their lifetime by His wise and loving counsel. 'Who hath directed the spirit of the Lord, or being His counsellor hath taught Him', Isaiah asks, and, 'With whom took He counsel and who instructed Him'.

Discounting these subjects as being appropriate, I turned my thoughts to the one consistent theme raised by friends and others, who, having read my first book, wondered how God was dealing with me since its completion in March 1994. What could I write which would benefit others and glorify my Lord? Nothing. My thoughts reminded me of how askew my thinking was when my mother died. I felt I reached the borders of Romanism. I could not conceive of her being in a place where she would not bear my burdens and pray for me constantly, as she had done all her life, and direct me by God's truth in matters of importance. Surely she would converse with her Lord in Glory about her only daughter? I had to cry urgently for forgiveness and ask Him to keep me from sinning in my grief. I knew from Scripture that the daughter/mother relationship ceased at death, but in that moment it was difficult to comprehend this. How were my faculties to grow in order that I might write that which would be authentic, inspirational, helpful and God given? By reading, observation, conversation, experience. Was this enough? Could I with honesty, knowledge and wisdom, write from my own experiences that which might benefit my fellow sufferer? Could I really say I bore my trials and afflictions with an even mind, enduring and persevering in all? By no means perfect, my imperfection would be written over all my work.

These musings led me to cry unto the Lord to guide me in all I wrote, to presence Himself in my thoughts, to give me a title for the book and appropriate headings for each chapter.

Chapter Two

Bethesda

---------------------- ❖ ----------------------

'An angel went down at a certain season into the pool.'
John 5:4

James, pen in hand, gazed with unseeing eyes through the open door, a familiar pensive look on his face as he struggled for that flash of inspiration which would give punch to his arguments. His submission must be watertight. The island community depended on the Health Board and its General Manager to get it right. The 'phone rang. There never was a right time for the 'phone to ring. "Rev. Macleod to speak to you", his secretary announced. The call concluded, James rose to his feet and stood momentarily at the window observing the traffic flow ceaselessly on the street below. "Coffee", he thought, but first he must call on the Chief Area Nursing Officer (C.A.N.O.) and advise her of Rev. Macleod's proposal.

"Are you free to attend a meeting next Tuesday with a sub-committee of the Free Church presbytery?", he asked. Affirming that I was we briefly discussed the way forward, as we saw it.

The press were mounting their strategy. They were not just interested in a story, they were interested in advancing a cause. Was it really the case that you could prise open an external wall of Block B, County Hospital with a pocket comb? One of the Officers had stated this at the last Board meeting. Surely this state of affairs would move the Scottish Office to accept the Board's submission and release the necessary capital funding?

In 1985, with twenty nine patients requiring to be decanted into temporary accommodation to allow urgent remedial work to take place, the headlines read: 'Disquiet over hospital beds', and later, 'Hospital beds crisis'. By the autumn of the same year acceptance was received to the twelve million pound 212-bedded development, but realisation of the facility would take several years.

In the meantime the sub-committee of the Free Church presbytery was discussing these local issues at their meetings. The other major presbyteries were already impacting on need, but it was obviously insufficient to meet the growing demands of the elderly population. Speaking with conviction the Rev. A.M. Macleod, after many consultative meetings, received the backing of presbytery to investigate with the Health Board ways of supplementing the unmet needs of the service. In that moment history was written.

Back at the Health Board offices the General Manager and the C.A.N.O. were discussing proposals for their meeting with the sub-committee of the presbytery. It was their opinion that the provision of nursing home accommodation with convalescent beds would alleviate the situation. This was a facility, readily available to mainland Boards, but which did not exist on the island at the time. The proliferation of privatised nursing homes within the country as a whole, was not foreseen. The proposal was therefore the more desirable.

While coming to the meeting with an open mind it was apparent that the sub-committee were considering the provision of residential beds with part nursing home accommodation. By the end of the meeting they agreed to convey to their presbytery the Board's proposal together with the outcome of their future meeting with the Social Work Department.

Two years previously, probably on account of my own experience with cancer, I was drawn towards the concept of hospice care. I had already discussed the viability of the project with Officers from Cancer Relief Macmillan Fund (C.R.M.F.), the Health Board and its Medical Committee. The scheme received their approval in principle. I began to develop a working strategy. Into this arena came Scottish Office approval to the Board's submission for a new hospital on a green field site. Work on the hospice had to be shelved. I found myself on the project team of the new hospital development.

As our meetings with the sub-committee continued and costings were prepared to assist them in their decision, a new thought was germinating in my mind. I discussed it with Tom Scott of C.R.M.F. and was encouraged. However, after the first flush of inspiration I began to doubt the wisdom of my thinking, until a fresh surge of adrenalin enabled me to approach the Chairman and ask if the presbytery would consider hospice provision as part of the nursing home development. 'For the vision is yet for an appointed time... though it tarry wait for it'. Agreement was given.

The project was finally launched in March 1989. Taking the scheme forward was a Management Committee comprising membership drawn from the other presbyteries and certain statutory and voluntary organisations. As the Health Board's nominee I found myself involved from an early stage.

The Committee's aim was to raise £700,000. A charitable collection was arranged on a door to door basis and approach was made to exiles living in America. Fundraising began in earnest. The public responded enthusiastically and in the first year contributed £180,000 to the fund.

As time went on building costs rose and the spontaneous liberality of the island population began to wane. The long step towards making the Home and Hospice a reality became wearisome. Action required to be taken. Finally, the Committee resolved to construct the building in two phases. The estimated cost of Phase I was £800,000, this meant there was a shortfall in cash terms of £500,000 and with a scheduled building programme of only thirteen months, it left little time in which to raise the required monies. Confident of the Lord's faithfulness and believing that the project was of Him, the Committee moved steadfastly on. The miraculous happened. Cash flowed in through donations, legacies and grants and the construction and furnishing costs were met as they arose. Bethesda opened its doors, free of debt on the 9th March 1992, proving conclusively that God never fails His praying people. He was there in the first conceptual thought. The project couldn't fail, His honour was at stake.

After nineteen months the Committee felt encouraged to proceed with the second phase. In arriving at their decision they took into account that even with hospice care free to the patient, income exceeded expenditure on a regular basis. The estimated cost for Phase II was £200,000 and in November 1993 the extra beds were commissioned free of debt. The total cost of the entire project was £1,088,000. This took account of construction, furnishings and equipment. A staggering sum for a catchment area of only 22,000 people and in an island community which saw a reduction of a major enterprise and the slump in the Harris Tweed industry. It was undoubtedly due to the generosity of islanders on both sides of the Atlantic as much as to grants, legacies and donations. It was a phenomenal achievement. A token of the Lord's bounteous provision.

The vision of the Chairman, Rev. A.M. Macleod, and his sub-committee of 1985 is now a reality. He promoted the development and saw it through to its functional stage. He encouraged his members by his personal commitment and faith. He believed the project was of the Lord and would be a lasting tribute to the One who alone can make all things possible.

Although in the providence of God I felt led to retire early from the Health Service, it was not with a view to working in Bethesda. Yet, when the post of Matron/Manager was advertised in September 1991, it was impossible not to apply. I prayed fervently over my decision and these words fell into my thoughts, 'Who is sufficient for these things?'. Was I? With my history of cancer I would have turned down my own application, but I knew I was surrounded by tokens of His care and I believed He would keep me in health to see Bethesda up and running. I knew I had the necessary skills and the necessary contacts to set up a new service. I believed that the eighteen years I worked as a nursing administrator with the local Health

Board was but the Lord's school of learning for this appointment.

Thus began the final years of my working life. Despite some pitfalls they were gloriously happy years. As the Lord, when He was on earth, walked among the poor at the pool of Bethesda, so He walks today among the sick and infirm in this modern complex. The environment may be different from the Jerusalem House of Mercy, but it is as vibrant with God's blessing as when the angel came down to disturb the pool. The atmosphere is restful and relaxed, affording patients and residents dignity and a quality of life as active as their circumstances permit. It is God who orders our habitation and in his mercy and grace He has appointed this unit as the final habitation for many of His children, souls who have already experienced the transition from time to Eternity. What a privilege to be associated with it and with all it stands for and be counted with those who try to alleviate the overwhelming feelings of powerlessness and the distressing symptoms which often herald death. To understand the responses of suffering loved ones and to address the needs of the frail elderly in care.

When I worked here I often identified with those in the hospice. I was one of them, suffering from the same disease but at a different stage. I did not impart this to patients but I observed their interaction with their disease and with their friends and relatives. How, I wondered, would I interact when my time came. I was often reminded I was but a creature of clay, living out the few short years of my sinful life. My best aspirations fell so far short of His word and I knew myself unworthy of the least of His mercies. As I witnessed my fellow beings called into Eternity I knew that it was by His command I came into being and that when His time came by the same command I would depart this life, not reluctantly but willingly, claiming the privileges of daughtership. How I longed for a deeper, purer relationship with Him so that living or dying I might serve Him.

On account of age and ill health I knew that my time in Bethesda would be short, but the inspiration I drew from working here gave every duty a purpose and mitigated the weariness of bodily affliction. It was an enabling factor helping me to bear pain with Christian fortitude and patience. Of myself I am nothing, but through His sufficiency I can do all things. How often I was to learn in my own experience that, 'Without me ye can do nothing'. By the same token, with me or through me you can do everything. By His grace on the 20th October 1995, I demitted office.

Chapter Three

God's Retirement Plan

❖

'Feed me with food convenient.'
Pro. 30:8

The finger of time advanced another few minutes on the clock of my earthly life and suddenly it made all the difference between being a working woman and being a retired person. I had been immersed in work continuously for forty one years. It had contributed greatly to the richness and happiness of my life. Could I in retirement achieve the same sense of purpose? Could I, with my health related problems, develop new pursuits, desirous only of fulfilling my Lord's bidding? I knew it was my duty as a Christian to make the best use of my time, talents and opportunities and I knew I would be held account-able for this in retirement as in working life. But what would the Lord have me to do? I still had no clear picture of my future, but I believed the cancer cells multiplying in my skeletal frame would not deter the outcome of His will for my life.

I had had plenty of time to consider my decision. I wasn't thrown into a 'grieving' situation as, perhaps, those in redundancy or in compulsory retirement might be. I could, therefore, look back with a sense of thankfulness and look forward, not with trepidation, but with a sense of stepping into the unknown, knowing that God knew the way and I had but to take my direction from Him. The day I left felt like a normal vacation except that some colleagues came to see me off. That was my first feelings of nostalgia. Going to Croatia helped, but my presentation on my return, with my successor in office, brought home the finality of my decision. Like the psalmist, I had to lift my eyes to the hill from whence my strength came and with confidence anticipate the unfolding of His retirement plan for my life.

I was soon to find out how easy it was for Satan to assail my peace of mind and in so many ways. He never retires but sometimes we forget this. John Newton, speaking of this enemy, aptly referred to his business as 'Satan, Self and Co.'. Seldom working alone, Satan engages self rather too easily, as I found out for myself. Spiritual warfare is very real, and alert to his machinations we must keep our armour on for he goes about as a roaring lion as well as an angel of light. He is intent on weakening our witness and rendering us ineffective through the many doubts with which he feeds our minds. But by trusting our Lord and clinging to Him, faith conquers.

Another assault I am conscious of is the way in which Satan allures my thoughts and conversation into worldly pastures on the Lord's Day. I normally spend this day in church, in the reading of material of spiritual wealth or listening to cassettes, but sometimes I find myself in uncontrolled fashion gazing idly into the fire. By the time I realise my folly I have attempted unimaginable feats. I must then call upon the Lord, seeking His forgiveness for the ways in which I have desecrated His day. Satan gives so many reasons or excuses as to why we should turn this day into an ordinary day. Even Christians fall into this trap, engaging in pleasures or work on His day which the Lord's command prohibits. His day is no ordinary day, it never was and never will be and His command admits no interpretation that weakens its authority. As someone once wrote, 'Things that disturb human arrangements are never justified in cancelling divine requirement'.

These circumstances intensified my longing to bring forth fruit with patience, to act from spiritual principles in all I might do and to esteem the importance of each day, remembering that in this new found state of retirement it might be easier to travel downhill rather than continue my journey with determination and purpose. Could I look forward, I questioned, with any degree of certainty? I had lived long enough to see generation follow generation so quickly. My own mortal existence was passing like a flash, the cares of the working life I knew over many years were now falling upon a rising generation. Simon Wastell, who died some three hundred years ago summed up man's mortality in the following words:

> 'Like to the grass that's newly sprung,
> Or like a tale that's new begun,
> Or like the bird that's here today,
> Or like the pearled dew of the May,
> Or like an hour, or like a span,

Or like the singing of a swan,
E'en such is man; - who lives by breath,
Is here, now there, in life, and death.
The grass withers, the tale is ended,
The bird is flown, the dews descended,
The hour is short, the span not long,
The swan's near death, - man's life is done'.

Notwithstanding my mortality, in Christ I live, move and have
my being and I can in dependence upon Him step forward
accepting as from His gracious hand whatever package He has
planned for my retirement years, few or many as those may
be.

So it was that I found my thoughts analysing todays
in-word, 'package'. In the caring services 'packages', be they
counselling or bereavement skills or whatever, are intended to
instruct and give guidance whereby quality can be improved. I
could only know what God's package for my retirement
included as His plan unfolded. Doubtless it would be
challenging, it would be of the highest quality, it would be
instructive, it would be directional, it would effect resignation
to His will and it would be food convenient to my soul. Might
it contain some surprises? I was sure it would. But whatever it
contained, it could only be very good, for this is how He
pronounces all that He does. How often had I planned, thinking that I covered every eventuality only to find in the course
of things new direction thwarting all my efforts. But God's
plan cannot be foiled. He ascertains what is beneficial for us,
bringing good out of our disappointments and testifying that
the way of a man is not in himself. His providence influences
and directs our thoughts and actions.

As I recollect my experiences since I retired I have to conclude that these, as surely as the dispensation of pain which walks with me by day and shares my bed with me at night, are instances of His providence. Pain, like my visit to Croatia, is a humbling experience. It cannot be shared or entered into by another. It isolates the individual, especially during episodes of extreme suffering, yet I have to confess it is an aid to spiritual growth, a means, to quote another, 'to keep me from losing my way to my heavenly rest'. Without this affliction I might become neglectful. The psalmist could say that, 'before I was afflicted I went astray, but now I have kept thy word'. I long to affirm that my experiences fall in line with this truth.

At present my tent is pitched in the field of retirement over which I will pass but once. I am already aware that my earthly tabernacle is coming down. Should I not, therefore, with great earnestness examine what influence my daily conduct has on this last phase of my life? Should I not give more heed to the fact that my Christian life is never retired and that I must endeavour to work for the Master while I can and not spend my days idly? Should I not store up Truth and knowledge and useful information which will be an adjunct in the valley of the shadow of death? Memory is an amazing power and this was brought home to me a number of years ago when I visited an elderly Christian lady in hospital. She had just been advised that her condition was irreversible, yet, she was fully reconciled to the outcome. More problematic to her was the fact that she could no longer read her Bible. This saddened her and as she shared with me how she took worship each day her words imprinted themselves on my mind. "Today", she said, "I am thankful for all the passages of scripture I was made to learn in day and Sunday school. I repeat these morning and evening before my prayers as my diet of worship". Does this not bring out clearly the value of storing Truth in our memory. It may be our only means of consolation in the final weeks of our lives.

The chapters which follow bring out the ways in which God's plan has unfolded in the brief time since I retired. There have been some surprises, but in the main it has been a time of chastening, of days and nights of pain, interspersed with periods of respite which were truly part of God's cup of blessing. There has been emotional suffering, unconnected with physical pain, but balancing this there has been broadened friendships. There has been a walk in the valley of weeping, but even here I found wells of living waters. As surely as God, by His grace, prepared me for retirement, so by His grace He has prepared me for the trials and blessings which are part of His lessons in grace. There is much I do not understand but do I require to understand it? Is it not sufficient that my Lord is at all times in control of every situation. His ways perplexed that holy man Job, he was to utter, 'It is God that maketh my heart faint and the Almighty that troubleth me'. Irrespective of what my cup contains I will never walk Job's experiences, yet, 'In all this did not Job sin with his lips'. Can I say that? Sadly not. What I can say is that He is faithful to His promise. 'He is a buckler to all those who trust in Him', and His grace is sufficient. Surely, therefore, this pilgrim, sometimes in the Valley of Achor with troubles arising from within and without and sometimes riding on the crest of the wave of His blessing, conscious only of the hope set before me, can trust the whole of my future to Him? Of course I can, and so Christian reader can you. We are anchored to the Rock of our salvation and, 'He that trusteth in the Lord shall be delivered'.

Chapter Four

Croatia

— ❖ —

'It is not in man that walketh to direct his steps'.
Jer. 10:23

"Haven't you heard that bombs are being dropped there?",
my friend asked in total disbelief that I was planning a visit to
Croatia. Actually peace had been restored, but politically
matters were still a bit fragile. When several friends expressed
astonishment I began to think there was something doubtful
about my attempt to visit this country and for fear that I might
lose my sense of individuality I ceased to make reference to
my holiday destination. It is clear that in this, as in other matters in my life, the Lord had planned according to His infinite
wisdom. It is more preferable that God rule our lives according to His counsel than that we ourselves might have choice in
the matter.

When one of my Welsh friends casually suggested that I accompany her on a visit to friends in Croatia, she immediately excited my interest. Exploring with her the date of this proposed event I discovered it coincided with the termination of my employment. The argument in favour took on a new dimension. And so it was that straight from work on my last day I flew into London. Next morning we boarded our Airbus bound for Zagreb.

The journey passed in uneventful silence. My friend, ear plugs tucked firmly into her ears, an abundance of sweets to hand, busied herself turning over the pages of the airlines 'Business Life' magazine. To anyone who has experienced a flying phobia these activities bespeak discomfiture. I should know, having spent many years of my working life distraught at the thought of a flight, especially to Uist, where in these early days the small 'Islander' was in use. What distressed me even more than my unfounded fears was the fact that I travelled mostly with persons who could not understand my plight and would often question how a Christian could be so distrusting. For years I prayed for the eradication of this crippling phobia without any seeming relief. Each time I required to leave Lewis, both my mother and a family friend prayed fervently for me.

My mother never forgot the occasion I accompanied her in the air ambulance to Inverness. It was an extremely windy day and we were tossed mercilessly seven thousand feet above the Minch. I was sure we would ditch. Fortunately the aircraft carried a doctor who attended to my mother's needs, while I, in paralysed fear, sat in the tail-piece seat praying over and over again, "Lord, take us there safely". Afterwards, my mother was to confess her own concern, for me, for the crew and for the doctor. She spent the journey praying that no lives would be lost on her account.

The first time I was required to fly after my mother's death I remember thinking, "Who will pray for me now?", and very interestingly from that time the Lord removed my fear. I cannot say that all my nervousness is gone, especially in adverse weather conditions, but fear as it was known to me then certainly has and I thank and praise God for His deliverance. It amazes me that cancer holds no anxiety for me and yet a journey by air could produce such intense and irrational feelings. I have never been able to comprehend this. I clung to Him in faith in both circumstances, His grace as sufficient in one as in the other, His steadfastness as immovable and yet when in flight His comfort denied. As I look back, I still cannot understand why on these occasions the fountain of life seemed to dry up. Perhaps I needed to learn that my sufficiency must be in Him alone.

This experience enabled me to commiserate with my friend in the quiet of my heart and as our aircraft lost height I could gaze over the new vista it afforded instead of sitting tensely with my eyes closed. In the warmth of the afternoon sun we disembarked and made our way to what seemed an empty airport building. The only passengers were those from our flight and those going to London on the return flight. We didn't see another civilian airline on the tarmac. Following hostilities, Zagreb Airport had only recently reopened.

The journey to our hotel took three hours but we saw little evidence of war. In the days which lay ahead, in many of the areas visited we saw great devastation. Having gone to Croatia with someone who had friends in the country meant we had the advantage of seeing and learning a great deal more than the average tourist. For me it was an entirely new experience, I had never been so close to a war zone since my childhood days in Glasgow.

On Sunday we worshipped in the Baptist Church. The service, which lasted two hours, was interpreted for our benefit by an English teacher who, with her husband, held high office in the communist regime. When communism fell in the former Yugoslavia, they lost all their possessions. Bitterness ensued but on a visit to Wales as interpreter to thirty refugees she came under the influence of the gospel. On her return to Croatia she came through to a saving knowledge of the Lord Jesus Christ.

When fighting broke out the pastor of this congregation became very involved with the innocent victims of the war. Grieved by all he saw he inspired church leaders and others to help. Together they set up an organisation known as 'my neighbour' where truckloads of foodstuffs and other commodities were received. We visited this large store and saw a team of volunteers from Canada sorting out packages of food in readiness for distribution. Potatoes seemed to be in great demand and while we were there sackloads were being allocated to those most in need. The whole operation was a hive of co-ordinated activity.

In this store we met a young mother and her child who, with many tears, shared with us her experience of living in a country at war. All her lifetime the two factions of the community had lived peaceably together, now there was distrust and open hostility. We came away in sombre mood.

The pastor's next project was to acquire a disused property, where he could bring groups of refugees together for respite care. A 'revolving door' system was introduced whereby refugees could return to the Centre from time to time as individual needs dictated. This sanctuary, based on Christian principles, and familiarly known as the Life Centre, accommodates forty four refugees at any one time. The aim is to restore mental and physical health and demonstrate the love of Christ. A service is held morning and evening which lasts for one hour. Christian videos are available for viewing throughout the day. Residents, while encouraged to attend, are not coerced to do so. We attended one service which was interpreted for our benefit, the central theme was peace.

As we spent a lot of our time among the refugees in the Life Centre we tried to communicate with them by touch and by smile. Those resident during our stay were a mixed elderly group whose average age we calculated as seventy five years. The men spent a lot of their time in the garden talking together while the women spent part of the afternoon in their bedrooms crocheting. What fun they had trying to teach us their intricate designs, but how sad to see them pull a handbag or a few photographs from under their pillow and with much talk point to this child or that house, obviously their grandchildren and their homes and then pathetically stretch out their arms in a gesture of hopelessness which said "they are no more".

With the Life Centre functional and meeting its objective, another property was purchased further along the road. This Villa, managed by a doctor who gave up her employment to work voluntarily with the refugee children, brings hope into the lives of youngsters whose sufferings are enormous. The first group to arrive came from Bosnia, while one of the more recent groups came from Sarajevo. Many had not seen the outside of their homes for about three years while others, having experienced the loss of family and friends, resided at refugee camps. Imagine their joy at being able to play freely outside and with each other. Things we take for granted.

Before leaving the country we had the privilege of viewing a large three storey dilapidated school building which had just been purchased for seven thousand pounds. A proportion of the capital costs of all these buildings came through donations received from various countries including America. Soft furnishings were received from Wales and beds were supplied by a Christian group in Sweden. I'm sure, like Scotland who donated the double glazed windows and sent a team to install them, other countries contributed, but these were especially mentioned. Viewing this building in its raw state one could be forgiven for thinking it was fit only for demolition. We were assured, however, that the Life Centre was once in a similar condition and that thirty volunteers made it habitable in three months. Following remedial work this building is expected to house war traumatised refugees who require longer term rehabilitation. It is expected that they will be taught new skills as part of their programme.

The users of these facilities, having had no one with whom to share their feelings and sufferings while in refugee camps are desperately lonely. They have lost loved ones and their homes and know not what their future holds or where it lies. In these Christian centres they appreciate having someone who will listen to them and try and sort out their problems.

What immediately strikes the visitor is the atmosphere of peace and of restfulness which pervades these centres. I likened it to Bethesda and there were several other similarities. As with Bethesda the Croatian centres were the vision of Christians and the church, they were set up on Christian maxims, are managed by Christian personnel and there is a diet of worship both ends of the day. The cardinal difference is the user. In Croatia the user is the victim of war.

We heard some wonderful stories of Christian love in the face of unspeakable atrocities, men and women who could confess to the profundity of what God had done in their hearts and lives, but we also heard some very very sad stories indeed. To relate all would be a book in itself. But, I cannot conclude without reference to one person whose selfless service to suffering humanity made a great impression on me and led to fundraising activities in Lewis and in a village in Wales.

The Life Centre is managed and directed by its founder, while an elder from the Baptist church, who gave up his job as a civil engineer to work voluntarily in this complex, is assistant director. His wife , a paediatric nurse, who also gave up her employment, works voluntarily in the laundry, washing the bed linen and the clothes of the refugees. She does this from morning to evening each day, excepting the weekend. Assisting her in this labour of love is one young volunteer who helps to hang out the washing and stretch the sheets before folding them away. There is one industrial washing machine, one domestic washing machine for personal items and one small domestic iron. When it is considered that she launders for eighty four residents, forty four adults and the forty children housed in the Peace Villa, one can envisage the mammoth task she undertakes. As I thought of the equipment for twenty five residents and patients in the Bethesda laundry and each item essential, I wondered how this poor woman, with twin sons aged eleven and a home to run, could ever cope - but cope she did. Voicing my concern I suggested we should try and help and on our return home the Croatian Laundry Appeal Fund was launched. It was not easy meeting the target and if the firm from whom the equipment was purchased had not assisted us with V.A.T. exemption and a good selling price, we might still be trying to raise funds. It was, therefore, a great joy when in

August 1996 the order for the equipment was finally placed.

While I was in Croatia I was experiencing a lot of pain. Several nights I sat in agony on the edge of my bed, swallowing analgesia and praying that the Lord would ease my condition and sustain me throughout the remainder of our visit, and He did. Whenever I returned home I saw my doctor and the next day boarded a 'plane for Inverness where I received a further scan and radiotherapy. I had planned a visit to West Africa, leaving in three weeks, but God overruled. Metastic disease and a fall on the ice put this visit outwith my reach, but I believed that in God's providence I would still be enabled to realise this childhood dream.

Chapter Five

Promoting Spiritual Growth

❖

'The branch cannot bear fruit of itself.'
John 15:4

The wheel of the lapidary revolved on its axle, cutting and grinding the precious jewel subjected to its motion until all that was worthless was removed and it shone with a brilliance it would never otherwise have known. Without the skilful touch of the lapidary the many facets of the diamond would never burn with its distinguished beauty, colour and perfection. A similar process is essential in the life of the believer until all that impedes growth and holiness is removed. Only then can the Lord's jewels shine brightly in the firmament for ever and ever. Is it presumptuous to regard my own pain and sufferings, which so often mars my comfort and detracts from the quality of my life, as being God's emissary summoned to do this work? I think not, for if I am truly His I must be separated from all my imperfections, until clothed in the beauty of holiness I am found fit to stand in His presence.

As a result of the fall affliction is the common lot of all mankind, but the Lord in His providence turns afflication to the good of the believer. Only then can it become a sanctifying process. Afflicted with cancer since 1979, I can certainly testify to the ways in which the Lord stood with me and strengthened me. In the fourteen months since I retired I have received radiotherapy on seven separate occasions. Mostly to my thoracic spine, where certain vertebrae, having collapsed, give rise to curvature of the spine and a distinctive stoop, but I have also had my jaw, skull and cervical spine irradiated. Prior to this my metastasis were contained in my pelvic region and for this I received treatment four times over a period of six years. I also had an attack of pericarditis. I state this simply to highlight the fact that through all the pain associated with my many metastasis the Lord has wondrously sustained me, directly through His word and indirectly through the prayers of His children. In my last book I made reference to my personal choice in the matter of drug administration. Now with much more experience of pain and suffering and in the receiving of hard drugs for the relief of chest pain, my choice remains unchanged. To me the side effects and the dulling of my powers of concentration outweigh the benefits. I hasten to emphasise that this is not something I recommend to others so afflicted. Intractable pain requires appropriate medication and we must thank the Lord that this is available to us, but for me, at present, excepting such a situation, I prefer to cast myself on the Lord's mercy and to trust Him in each separate experience. Through prayer, the aid of moderate analgesia and an increasing pain threshold the Lord has hitherto helped me. At this stage in my illness quality of life is of supreme importance and I thank the Lord I have this in measure. I can still go to church, except during painful episodes, enjoy the company of friends, read, write and, to a lesser extent, travel. For these multitudinal blessings I wish I had a thousand tongues to praise the Lord. This is not to say I have never known moments when I longed to be released, when I felt worthless and a burden to friends and carers, but even in these situations I can reflect upon the Lord's sustaining grace.

In December 1995 I found myself, yet again, in hospital in Inverness. Normally, I receive radiotherapy as an outpatient, but either way it necessitates a trip to the mainland of Scotland. When in hospital, I write my thoughts each day, oftentimes in the form of a prayer. A few of these jottings I share with you:

'19:12:95 Pain washes over me ... May it effect soul cleansing ... Lord, teach me acceptance, resignation, obedience, patience, contentment, godliness.

20:12:95 Lord, in my state of pain and discomfort would that I might understand thy teaching. That I might be still and know thy salvation, that I might be in constant communion with thee, listening to all that thou art saying ...

20:12:95 Oh! Lord help me to bear this pain with Christian fortitude. Help me to love thy dealings with me, to recognise thy chastening, to draw comfort from thy truth. 'My son, despise not thou the chastening of the Lord, nor faint when thou art rebuked of Him ...'. I long for illumination, to know where this pain is leading. I long for human companionship, the touch of a hand and someone to speak of the Saviour's love. Am I going to get over this pain, even partially, or am I being asked to receive it as a token of love, cleansing and preparing me for that great Day? Be with me during my journey to Wales.

24:12:95 Through this affliction may I have a better understanding of myself and the praiseworthy God who is always a step ahead, who knows what He is doing and who from eternity knew the outcome. Teach me Lord to say, 'Amen', in every circumstance.

25:12:95 Christmas day in Wales. Still find it painful to move or lift my bag off the floor. It is early days. Another week before I know whether radiotherapy will help .... Lord, I would like to live a little longer. I haven't lost the zest for work, especially in thy cause.... My faith is being tested. Oh! for complete submission to thy will. If I am to live with pain for the remainder of my life may it be at all times to thy glory. Oh! to be conscious of thy love, were it to blossom in my heart it would make my pain ever so easy to bear.

26:12:95 Cast me in the mould of thy choice and sustain me by thy grace. Thank you, Lord, for friends who have taken me into their homes and their hearts. Make it up to them a thousand fold in spiritual blessings. When times of affliction overtake them, be close to them Lord, easing every heartache and every discomfort. Help them to embrace thy will and to bear whatsoever cometh from thy hand.'

On the twenty seventh I left Wales and spent a night at Inverness on the way home. My pain was still rather uncomfortable and I saw the Oncologist before returning to the island. He assured me that given time there would be a seventy per cent improvement in my condition, but this was not to be the case. It was but the beginning of my spinal problems. I never questioned the Lord's dealings, I trusted Him and knew He didn't require to justify what He was doing.

I have always been kept well informed as to the progress of my disease. I know I am being treated palliatively and not with a view to cure. This holds no fear, living or dying I believe I am His and going over bone or C.T. scan results or x-rays with the Consultant, tells me less than my Lord already knows. Before I had being He knew the course my disease would run and it only remains for me to prayerfully await the outcome.

As the New Year of 1996 was heralded in, my thoughts returned to Africa. I so much wanted to go and having considered all my health problems the desire remained. Would I be well enough to go in May? I spoke often to the Lord about it and came to the conclusion I shouldn't delay my visit. Could this be another of God's retirement surprises? 'Be still and know that I am God'. I waited on the Lord to make the desire a reality.

Before my visit to Africa, the decision was taken to refer me to the pain clinic in Glasgow for nerve block intervention. I was not too troubled about this procedure, having committed the concerning elements to the Lord, instead I turned my thoughts to the mystery of providence. Why was I being sent to this clinic? Did the Lord want me to share my faith and the marvellous outworkings of cancer in my life? I prayed for the opportunity to witness and began to look forward to my visit. Laying aside the preliminaries, the decision was taken that I wasn't a suitable candidate for this procedure, but over the months I attended the clinic the Lord enabled me each time to share freely with those present all that was on my heart.

The night before I left for Glasgow I experienced quite disabling pain. As I lay awake I remember thinking, as I had on other occasions, "I'll never be able to travel like this". I considered the advantages of belonging to a family, at least I could expect someone to accompany me. Into my troubled thoughts fell the reference to Elijah when, on God's instruction, he was fed by the ravens. Surely, I thought, God could provide a 'raven' for me or give respite from pain, making my journey comparatively easy? And this is exactly what He did. There are times when I feel the Lord is giving me Benjamin's portion, a double blessing. Not only did He take me to Glasgow, but I slept that night and awoke refreshed, with the glorious words of the psalmist on my lips,

'And in God's house forever more,
My dwelling place shall be'.

A wonderful peace permeated my being, warming my heart and emotions. Whether death was imminent or in the distance I was to dwell in His house forever. What blessed assurance filled my soul.

Night pain seems twice as difficult to bear, especially when one is alone. I think this is why the Lord gives songs in the night. I recall quite intolerable pain one night when I told the Lord I could no longer bear it. With persuasive power He spoke these words into my soul, 'when thou passest through the waters I will be with thee and through the rivers they shall not overflow thee'. How I thanked the Lord for his overtures of love. The following morning as I thought over these words, tears coursed down my cheeks. Were they numbered among the tears to which Spurgeon referred as 'the diamonds of Heaven?'. I know not, but they were certainly tears of tenderness.

Of all the pain I have so far experienced, excepting my chest pain, I think the last occasion was the severest. Perhaps this is an illusion. When relief comes I tend to forget the severity of previous pain. This time pain presented as I was writing. My arm and especially my elbow was so acutely painful that I groaned as I wrote. "Lord, help me", I prayed, "or I will never conclude this book". A few days later I was back in Inverness. For about three weeks I could not write, read or concentrate. For the first time I never sought friends, never asked for prayer, except the evening before I returned from Inverness, and wanted to be left alone. I have never fully understood my reaction. Prayer was difficult, that is until the evening pain reached its zenith and I thanked God for preserving my sanity. I felt His doing so stemmed from His infinite love. At the time I never knew myself to be in Warburton's company who, when on his death bed, was made to cry out; "Do keep me in my senses. I hang on thee like a cup on a nail, what a God thou art", nor did I know, until much later, that my simple prayer that night was replicated in greater detail in Spurgeon's autobiography. I was encouraged by these references. On the night to which I allude I cried to the Lord in a manner to which I was not accustomed. I reminded Him that He was my Father and I was His child, that He had promised to be Father to the fatherless, I reminded Him how I had no one to help and I knew Him to be the help of the helpless. I continued to speak with Him at this simple level until my pain eased sufficiently to ensure at least a broken night's sleep.

Speaking of his season of suffering, Spurgeon had this to say, 'I wrestled with God in what proved to be a crisis, locked with pain to an extreme degree, I could no longer bear it without crying out. I asked all to leave the room. I then had nothing to say to God but this, "Thou art my Father and I am thy child and as a Father thou art of tender mercy. I could not bear to see my child suffering as I am and if I did I would do what I could to help him. Wilt thou hide thy face from me, my Father, wilt thou still lay on thy heavy hand and not give me a smile from thy countenance". I pleaded the Fatherhood of God in earnest. Like as a father pitieth his child. When the family came in I ventured to say, "I shall never have such agony again from this moment for God heard my prayer". Ease came, the racking pain never returned. When we are lowest and very weak we can still say, "Father help me, Father rescue me."' On reading this I felt assured that my own simple approach accorded with scripture. I would without hesitation plead thus again.

Thinking over these situations I wondered if my reliance on the power of God to relieve and sustain would be the same if I was relying on strong medication. I can only know this if in the future I require the administration of drugs. The night I offered up that prayer from a heart crushed by pain I seriously thought for the first time of taking morphine, but the more I considered it the more I felt something holding me back. I certainly had relief to look forward to if my radiation was successful, fifty to eighty per cent I was told, and so I could tolerate each day with God's help. Spurgeon and kindred others were less fortunate. Spurgeon's case did not call for radiotherapy but even if it had he would have been unlikely, in that era, to receive it. He was certainly on medication, blue pills and a black draught, whatever that contained. By comparison with our suffering forebears, we are a truly privileged people. Help, in a variety of ways is available when we require it.

I cannot but marvel at the way in which the Lord has transformed my self-reliance and my attitude to my condition, it underlies every stage of my experience. By His grace I know contentment and patience and by His grace He meets my every need and enables me to say in the words of another, 'Lord, I am pained but I resign to thy superior will'. This is not to say that I do not encounter loneliness or feelings of wistful longing for a measure of health or a host of emotions in minor refrain. Resignation does not come naturally but He makes a willing people in the day of His power. It is required of us to take up our cross and follow Him and it is, therefore, better, as Spurgeon would say, to have our cross sanctified than have it removed. How insignificant my trials by comparison with the Lord's sufferings. His physical pain on the cross was so excruciating as to be incomprehensible to us and while our trials are graven in love all He received on the cross was vinegar to drink. And who can follow the Apostle Paul in his sufferings, even if he had the satisfaction of knowing his tribulations were on account of the gospel, it was still hard for his human heart to bear. Through his sufferings he learned contentment and the promise of the sufficiency of His grace, 'My grace is sufficient for thee: my strength is made perfect in weakness'. It was then he could say, 'Most gladly therefore will I glory in my infirmities'. May this be my experience.

As I journey on I count it a privilege and a blessing to have friends who have not tired of me, who shed the sympathising tear, who bear me faithfully to His throne and pray specifically when pain is at a premium. Surely, He who ordereth aright our life and our conversation and doth all things well, balances accurately our blessings and our sufferings? My outlook has absolutely nothing to do with me but everything to do with Him. Attitude, contentment and patience are all of grace.

Among the blessings shared and the many not shared, I number God's provision in keeping from me the experience of those whose reaction of loss in the face of terminal illness is very real. I heard of someone who on being advised of his terminal state faced his mortality with feelings akin to grief. What might you ask, could a dying man grieve over? Much, there is the loss of human faculties, the parting from loved ones and all that made up living, the loneliness, the vulnerability, the insensitive attitudes, the uselessness, the increasing dependence and finally the separation of life itself. There are numerous decisions to be made and for someone living on these islands, livestock may have to be sold or a faithful sheepdog found a home. These may seem trivia but they bring their own poignancy. The person to whom I refer on leaving his sheepdog with a friend returned home with feelings which were both painful and sad. Do we expect reactions such as this from someone prepared to meet death or someone fully aware that the autumn of his or her years knows no repeating? There is much evidence to substantiate this kind of reaction, but for the believer there is recovery, not the recovery associated with bereavement, which time will lessen, but the recovery which comes through wholeness in Christ and the imperative command, 'Come for all things are now ready'. Dr. John Ker, is quoted as saying, "It is not when our affections are heavy and fresh that we derive much benefit. We are stunned. It is afterwards that they yield the peaceable fruits of righteousness".

The grinding stone and the pruning knife are necessary to grind away the rough edges and to remove the useless branches in the believer's life. It is a painful process but necessary if the believer is to yield spiritual growth. By these means the heavenly Lapidary parts us from the worthless dross of our lives thus accomplishing within us a work which will enable us to burn with sanctified brilliance. Only then will his jewels, fit for a kingly crown, be gathered into His Kingdom and take their place among those already within the veil.

When through fiery trials thy pathway shall lie,
My grace all-sufficient shall be thy supply,
The flame shall not hurt thee: I only design,
Thy dross to consume and thy gold to refine.

Chapter Six

Africa Realised

❖

'Is there any thing too hard for me?'
Jer. 32:27

It was 8.20 a.m., our flight from Glasgow had just arrived in Brussels and we had well over five hours to wait before commencing the next lap of our journey. The airport, bustling with business men and professionals, briefcase in hand, had an air of prosperity. Where had they come from and where were they going? Who could tell, their faces gave nothing away. Observing fellow passengers, reading and chatting whiled away the first two or three hours, after that time seemed to stand still, that is until I noticed, sitting two seats along, a young man engrossed in his Bible. My friend engaged him in conversation and we learned that he was a believer, that he came from Russia and having been expelled from university on account of his faith, was now studying in Germany. A fluent German speaker, he preached in the local Baptist church in his university town. Over coffee we heard much about life in Russia, the poverty and the concerning aspects of the development of the church since the fall of communism. The next two hours flew by and as we parted we were conscious of the divine providence which brought us together in the middle of Brussels airport and of the unlikely event, although we exchanged addresses, of ever meeting again. It made a deep impression upon us.

Reflecting on the promptings which led to this journey, I recalled how forty four years previously, at the impressionable age of sixteen, I was reading a book about missionary endeavour in Africa. Immediately my imagination formed a vivid picture of the scene and by the time I finished the book my life's work was sealed; or so I thought. But, 'My thoughts are not your thoughts', saith the Lord. For six years my yearning to be a missionary in Africa remained unfulfilled. I wanted to go but I was held back, I never could enter into the depths of Rowland Hill's call, when he said, "Oh! that I were all heart and soul and spirit to tell the glorious gospel to the perishing multitudes". Had I known such fire I would have been certain of the Lord's calling, but in the absence of positive guidance and with providence dictating another path, I had to accept the Lord's ruling in the matter. But I never forgot Africa and now, with eternity looming ever nearer, I am overwhelmed by the fact that I have done nothing useful in the Lord's service. Missionary work continues to draw me, though not in the same simple way as in my early childhood, when I challenged someone thirty years my senior with the fact that she never attended church. In my zeal I believed, as I confronted her objection by going home and obtaining a hat for her, that she was bound to succumb. The disappointment when she didn't was acute, but at the time I knew not the significance of the words, 'Without me ye can do nothing'. Distributing tracts in Glasgow was another salutory lesson. No one was interested but still I couldn't give up.

These events were well in the past when I attended a Worldwide Evangelisation for Christ (W.E.C.) holiday in Switzerland. Little did I realise as I left Lewis the far reaching consequences of this vacation. Addressing the missionary session, Isa Arthur shared with us her work in Guinea Bissau. Enthralled, the old enthusiasm returned. Leafing through a British Airways map on the way home I eventually found the location of this republic which I had never even heard of until then. A firm conviction took hold that I would visit this mission station sometime in the future. I never thought eight years would pass, nor that my health would be so precarious, before I eventually accomplished my aspiration. Isa was aware of my medical history but she never discouraged me from my quest.

When local friends heard of my proposed visit, they expressed concern. The journey was long, four flights from Stornoway to Bissau with an overnight stop at Dakar in Senegal. How would I manage on my own? In response I began to pray for a companion and when exactly two weeks before I was due to leave a friend telephoned indicating her willingness to accompany me I took it to be an answer to prayer. Never have I known so many immunisations and vaccines administered at the same time. This was necessary to meet the requirements of the cover period and amazingly reaction was minimal. When the Lord effects His plan everything falls into place.

Dakar airport was the complete antithesis of Brussels. Dry, dusty, colourless, with lots of garbage on either side of a poorly surfaced runway. Despite those observations it was an incredible sensation to stand on African soil. Not since my visit to the Holy Land did I have such feelings of elation. The simple airport building was teeming with African porters, vying with each other over luggage and making it difficult for passengers to handle their own cases. We appreciated the hotel minibus which awaited our flight and tired and weary, but extremely thankful for God's protection and safety, we arrived at our hotel.

The air tickets for our flight to Bissau required to be purchased locally. Isa had sent these on to the Agency in Dakar, faxing the details before we left. Unfortunately our hour of arrival meant this office was closed and it was not open by the time we required to leave in the morning. There was nothing we could do but return to Dakar airport without a ticket for our onward journey. Explaining our plight to two French speaking Africans and making no progress we were eventually referred to a very helpful official who, on hearing of our situation and reading Isa's fax, issued us with boarding passes. What a relief. With only three flights a week we would have had to remain another two days in Dakar. We certainly evidenced the Lord's care toward us and so did the missionaries when their two excited guests arrived without a ticket.

The flight to Guinea Bissau took one hour. We were surprised to find we were not the only English speaking passengers. Guinea Bissau is not exactly tourist country and for a few minutes I pondered over the goal and final destination of these four people. Soon we heard the engines change and as we descended we had our first glimpse of the country which until then was merely a name. I don't know what I imagined but the reality was very different. The runway was a big improvement on Dakar, large and newly tarmaced, but the red arid soil and the tired looking trees called out for the rainy season. Descending the aircraft steps, the dominant heat of which we had heard so much hit us, but we ignored this as we entered the small terminal building and looked around for a glimpse of Isa. Warmly welcomed, we set off for the mission compound. On being introduced to the team leader, in whose home we were to sleep, we went across to Isa's house. The hens pecking the dry soil and friendly green lizards scurrying about were all part of our induction to Africa.

Guinea Bissau itself is a small West African republic of about a million people. It is one of the poorest countries in Africa. Since independence in 1974 the government has attempted to set up a more comprehensive education system for all children and also an improved health programme. The country is heavily dependent on overseas financial and technical aid for its development programmes. Industry is sparse and this presents a big problem as few young people find any kind of employment.

A tribal country, Guinea Bissau has about twenty three different tribes residing there. The ones the missionaries are mostly in contact with are the Fulas, muslim, but open to the gospel; the Mandingas, muslim, but harder to win for Christ. The two missionaries who work with this tribe have not seen any Mandingas truly come to the Lord in the eight years they have lived among them, even although they are permitted to evangelise openly. The Biafadas, Moncanhas, Nalus and Susus are all being reached. Those working among them, while helping in the churches, are mainly engaged in evangelistic work. In addition there are many anamists. They hold fetishes and believe in witch doctors in accordance with the traditional African religion. It would have taken a much longer period than our brief holiday to have understood how the missionaries relate to so many tribes, but what we were able to grasp fascinated us and revealed a large workload and a high missionary profile.

It is impossible to write on the whole visit in one chapter, but there are some unforgettable experiences, commencing with the simple duty of ablution. With the exception of the heat, it so reminded me of my early childhood in rural Lewis, in fact the missionaries were slightly better off, they at least had toilets and kitchen sinks, even if they didn't have running water, we had neither. It is amazing how much we can do without and still achieve the same result. Showering and toilet flushing was by means of plastic jugs of water, yet, surprisingly, this proved quite adequate. Night falls about 6.00 p.m. and by 7.00 p.m. when the compound generator is switched on it is quite dark. After 10.00 p.m. and through to 7.00 a.m. a torch or candle is necessary. The local electricity supply is very erratic and cannot be relied upon, an inconvenience to the missionaries dependent on computers for literacy and translation work.

Our first Lord's Day was an incredible experience. We were taken by truck to Bissalanca, a journey of about twenty minutes, to a small pastorless church where two different tribes worshipped together. We were warmly received and after the preliminary introductions a hymn was announced. The vigorous singing was unaccompanied but soon the congregations exuberance gave way and everyone clapped in perfect harmony. That small group of about thirty five Africans sang so lustily and with such feeling it brought tears to my eyes. I wish our congregations could muster so much joy in their singing. There were two short sermons, each interpreted for the benefit of the tribal languages represented. This was followed by prayer. The leaders advised their people of matters requiring prayer and the congregation prayed simultaneously. It was most orderly. Everyone commenced at the same time, reached a crescendo together and in unison tapered off. The whole service lasted three hours. Not long, when it is considered that one missionary was in a service which lasted eight hours. Much of this time was given over to fasting and prayer. As we left the church and spilled into the hot sunshine we were joyfully hugged as sisters in Christ.

The church building was constructed of red mud bricks and had a corrugated iron roof held in place by rafters made from tree trunks. The floor was of dry loose mud and the broad form-like seats and pulpit platform was of baked mud, piled to the appropriate height. The surface of the seats were highly polished but they lacked any back support, fortunately Isa had taken a chair along and I was able to sit comfortably during the service. The improvised pulpit was an oil barrel turned upside down and on this rested the Bible. To this simply furnished church the people travelled far distances, some quite severely physically handicapped, to hear the Word of God. Mothers nursed their babies openly but nothing detracted from the sermon or the tangible atmosphere. These poor people cannot afford to support a pastor, but during the rice harvest they tithe and bring their offering to God's house. Poor, maybe, but Oh! so rich. We felt very lowly as we returned to the mission compound.

Isa, having taken much needed time off, was able to show us around and introduce us to missionary colleagues in some of the villages. These visits were a revelation. Often at some distance from Bissau, we rattled along roads which were non existent, weaving our way in an effort to avoid the largest pot holes and the deep ruts of the mud tracks, with little respect for the highway code. All the drivers we met drove their vehicles in like fashion. On the way to Lendem it wasn't just the road conditions or the heat we had to contend with, it was the bridges of simple wooden planks. No room for a mistake, the wheels must remain on the narrow planks strategically placed on either side.

Our overnight visit to Lendem was full of interest. We had previously met Duncan, the Scottish Tear Fund worker based here and he had prepared a meal of haggis and potatoes for us. What could be more Scottish? But before our meal he must first dispose of a nest of rats in the living room and after the meal hasten off to visit a farmer who had suffered the loss of ten cows. It was late when he returned, having immunised all the remaining cattle and advised the farmer that he had an outbreak of anthrax and many more cattle would succumb before the morning. As we prepared for bed that night, my friend tucked the mosquito net firmly under the mattress to keep out the rats and the large red spiders which sped with astonishing alacrity across the floor. Despite their haste they didn't escape a swipe of Isa's Daily Telegraph. Was this why we took it with us? The mosquitoes took second place in our thoughts that night. Next morning we set off for Bissau, stopping at Bafata on the way. This was a very long journey but after lunch and siesta with Meta Dunlop, we felt refreshed for the next lap. Meta lives in the heart of an African village. With little privacy and no space she is surrounded by numerous African families, whose children wander into her home. How she loves the people of this Mandinga tribe. She holds a very large Sunday school and finds the children receptive, learning Scripture passages easily by heart. Saying our farewells we took our leave for the three hour journey back to Bissau. The only event on the way back was the inevitable puncture. However, two kindly Africans assisted us and within twenty minutes we were back on the road.

In addition to evangelism, the missionaries are heavily involved with literacy work and Bible translation which can take years to complete. The New Testament in the Papel language has just been received. This is the fruit of Lily Gaynor and her helpers. The Papels are slow learners and a desire to read the Word of God in their own language is prayed for. The Gospel of Luke and the Book of Acts, the work of Thelma Mills, is awaited in the Balanta language. But it is to the work of Isa Arthur that the church in Guinea Bissau owes most. She translated the New Testament into the Creole language some years ago and a reprint, expected when we were there, is now available and selling well. Since then she has translated the Old Testament into the same language and this has now been sent for type-setting. She is still working on some corrections. What must it be like to proof read a first translation of the Bible? Fortunately computers do much of this work today and discrepancies are more readily ascertained. Nonetheless Isa Arthur is known to have read through the whole of the Creole Bible seven times. This is no mean feat. Her dedication to her translation work and all that pertains to the peoples among whom she has laboured for forty years knows no telling.

In the early days of her missionary life Isa worked on the Bijagos Islands. While there she took over the care of a thirteen year old boy who lived with her for several years. Today Papa is a pastor, serving among his own people. We had the privilege of meeting him and his bond with Isa was very obvious. He speaks and reads English and took worship with us in our own language. A married man, he has three children and

Isa features strongly in this family unit. My health prevented us from undertaking the five hour sea crossing to these islands, but we did see Papa off and it gave us some insight into what could be expected. Isa herself is the best person to illustrate a journey on this boat. "It is a bit choppy but not too rough, which is fortunate for the canoes which have come out from the shore of the Island of Chickens, to bring and fetch passengers who climb up on board with babies and luggage while others climb down. Other passengers help, and one man is dangling a struggling, squawking chicken by the legs, waiting for the owner to take care of it. The boat is pretty full, the deck a sea of people and baggage. I'm sitting on a cool box while Hazel Wallis is sitting on her bucket, which has a good lid and is probably more practical than a suitcase when there are no seats on board. Its pretty cramped, as a confirmed optimist, I thought we wouldn't have people always squeezing past us. After all these years I still underestimate people's capabilities and determination. They struggle past, in front of me and behind Hazel, and somehow step around our luggage which is a fair pile. Behind Hazel sits a lady who has eggs in a frail plastic bag at her feet. So far with precautions taken by her, and me when she dozes off, nobody has stepped on them. Conversation means shouting into ears because of the noise of the engine. Many sit on the rails around the deck, with those embarking from canoes making their way along the outside of the rail. Four cows stand in a row along the rail on the other side. There is one toilet on board, the door of which seems to close with great skill and effort. When not closed the door swings back and blocks a narrow passage beside the staircase ....". I can see why it was decided that this adventure may prove too much for me, but I am amazed at what, with the Lord's help, I was actually able to achieve. It was exactly what I had imagined missionary life in Africa to be and every moment was filled with wonderment.

As we took our leave David prayed with us and Margaret, Thelma, Gertrude, Helga and Angela came to see us off. During our brief time in Guinea Bissau they shared their lives with us and we left with the impression of a truly dedicated team. Of course there will be difficulties and frustrations, but as in the past the Lord will see them through. For me the simple style of living, the sharing, the vibrant companionship, the warmth evident among the missionaries and the already mentioned hens and the little green lizards, are all part of an unforgettable experience. I would have liked to have stayed if I was in normal health, but I am not and so I must live on the memories and trust that God may grant me one further visit before He calls me Home. 'Not my will but thy will be done'.

Chapter Seven

The Belem Church

❖

'Remember the poor'.
Gal . 2:10

During our visit to Guinea Bissau Isa shared with us the difficulties facing the Belem Evangelical Church in Bissau in their struggle to complete their new church. Two years previously the congregation, after many years of selfless labour, completed the walls of the building, but there was no money left to roof it. Those concerned worked very hard to increase their givings, but the project was just too large for them. The four bare walls was in danger of becoming a timeless memorial to their concerted efforts.

The Evangelical Church of Guinea Bissau was established in the early forties through the work of W.E.C. International and the Belem Church was built in 1947. As a consequence of its outreach programme it has grown steadily and now has a congregation of three hundred members and adherents. Worshipping, as a temporary measure, in a very flimsy and totally inadequate structure, they are urgently in need of their new church. Each day while in Bissau we could see this ghost building of four walls, yet, though sympathetic towards the plight of the congregation, it never occurred to me to assist in any way.

The pastor of the church, on learning of our visit, extended, through Isa, an invitation to us to visit him. When we arrived he was out visiting and so we wandered towards the temporary church building next door. Even to our unskilled eyes it seemed in danger of collapsing, yet, within, a very enthusiastic group of young people were singing. When the pastor joined us he gave us a cordial welcome, spoke a few words through Isa and offered a prayer in the parting. He came across as a warm, loving Christian, committed to the work of his church and his evangelistic programme. It came as no surprise to learn of his pastoral duties, his visitation of the sick or to hear the children chant, "Pastor, Pastor", as he accompanied us to the car. Before we left we decided to worship, the following Lord's Day, at one of his outlying churches where he was to hold a service of dedication and communion. Another new experience for us.

Because of a slight uncertainty as to where the church was located, we left early, and having parked our car by the roadside, walked the short distance along the mud baked track to the church. The building, by contrast with the previous church building, was quite smart with simple church furnishings, nonetheless to ensure my comfort the deck chair went with us.

In front of me in his wheelchair sat a young handicapped man. I remember thinking how fortunate I was in having a disease which, so far, permitted me the liberty to walk. The service opened with singing and although hearty, for me, it was not in the same league as the singing we heard at the first church we worshipped in. Between sixty and seventy persons were present, all smartly dressed and with an eagerness to worship God. After an appropriate reading the five sets of parents with their children were called to the front. They were closely questioned by their pastor and after what appeared to be a lecture of some determinable length they were allowed to return to their seats. The service which followed was very searching, dealing with matters such as the requirement to bring their children up in the nurture and admonish of the Lord, to bring their children with them to God's house, to hold family worship and include their children, and, according to biblical injunction, the need to discipline and how this discipline ought to be administered. Following a prayer and singing this part of the service concluded. A communion address was then given on the words, 'This do in remembrance of me', after which the Lord's supper was dispensed. After all those years it was wonderful to find myself seated at the Lord's table with African brothers and sisters. The whole service lasted two and a half hours. That evening, our last in Bissau, the pastor called to see us and on being asked if he would share his testimony with us, we heard an amazing account of God's dealings with him from youth until he entered the ministry. His face shone as he concluded with the words, "I don't think the Lord can love anyone as much as he does me". And he meant it. Full of compassion and love he hugged us as we left, but more importantly, he prayed. We never understood a word, yet, that prayer was so obviously sincere it made a great impression upon us. It is not possible to tell whether we shall ever meet again on earth, but we can anticipate meeting in eternity.

About two months after my return to Lewis, quite suddenly and without explanation I found myself burdened on account of the Belem church. The burden continued. What could I do to help? The fundraising appeal for Croatia was coming close to target, should I launch another appeal so soon? The matter was decided for me. I found when I spoke with individuals about this needy cause, the money flowed in and so with the help of the local radio station and the Stornoway Gazette, the community were informed and an account opened at the end of August 1996 at one of the local Banks. By November the account was closed and £5,404, earmarked for this project, was sent to W.E.C. Headquarters in London. The amazing thing about the appeal was how effortless it proved. Even before I spoke with individuals or small groups, the Lord was opening hearts in a big way. Two elderly ladies on reading the local paper telephoned me. They were convinced the project was of the Lord and wanted more information. They then sent two substantial donations. Sunday schools, individuals and groups contributed. The largest donation came through a couple I had the opportunity of sharing with. I had only met them briefly in the past and when the following morning I learned of their decision, I was deeply moved. But of all the remarkable circumstances associated with this appeal I think the incident surrounding my visit to the pain clinic in Glasgow was the most extraordinary. Unable to find accommodation I changed my appointment and consequently my flight. Sitting beside me on the aircraft was a local business man. We chatted and on being asked what I was doing in retirement I replied that I was trying to roof a church in Africa. Thinking he would be disinterested I did not enlarge much upon it and so I was quite surprised when he handed over a cheque for £500. Had I not required to change my appointment I would never have met this gentleman, nor received his gift. The Lord's timing is meticulous. He makes no mistakes.

Quite unbeknown to me until after the account was closed, the Regional Co-ordinator for W.E.C. Ireland was also burdened about this church and he had set up a fund in Belfast. On learning, through Isa, of our fundraising efforts he contacted me. As a consequence all essential roofing materials are to be purchased and prepared in Ireland and shipped out by container. A small team of workers from Ireland are to go out in the Spring of this year (1997) to help with the steel erection and roofing. Another team are to go out in September to undertake the electrical work. God works in a mysterious way and I believe He took me to Africa so that, among other things, our island community might share in the completion of this new church, expected to accommodate eight hundred people. It is our prayer that God's spirit will richly bless the efforts of His people through an outpouring of His spirit in revival. In a recent letter from Isa, she confirmed that the people are really thrilled with this rich provision while the pastor, Quintino Gomes, writes, 'please convey our very sincere thanks to those who have given so generously. It's almost unbelievable that all this money should come to us from people we don't know personally. Words are inadequate but please tell them how grateful we are'.

In conclusion, it might be of interest to readers to know that since the Fellowship of the Evangelical Church of Guinea Bissau was first established through W.E.C. International, forty seven churches, together with numerous smaller groups who meet in homes and on verandahs, are active in the province. There are twenty seven pastors and a total attendance of ten thousand. Over 70% are under the age of twenty five years. The churches are mainly among the Balanta, Papel, Bijago and Manjaco tribes. In addition the Evangelical Church has its own Bible Training Institute. The salutation in the Creole language, 'Deus ta guarda bos' - 'May God keep you', is our prayer.

Chapter Eight

Sundry Situations

❖

'Who is the health of my countenance, and my God.'
Psa. 42:11

'St. James' Palace', read the envelope. I knew its
contents before I opened it. The Investiture was to take place
on 12th November 1996, but in the meantime I had an
appointment with the Oncologist, who confirmed metastasis
of the skull and jaw. He could treat both these areas, but he
again confirmed that nothing further could be done for my upper
spine. This was the region where my pain was most acute,
but I had to accept the outcome. Learning that hair loss was
inevitable as a consequence of radiation, it was agreed to leave
this area untreated until the week prior to my visit to London.

As this visit loomed nearer so my anxiety grew. How could
I go to London in my present state of health? Friends were

concerned for me and began praying in earnest for complete healing. One friend, attending a healing service, went forward on my behalf but I had no knowledge of this until after the event. So ignorant was I of healing services I never knew 'transference' was practiced. Other friends made like endeavours exhorting me to seek anointing with oil from my own minister, but as Matthew Henry puts it, '... the saving of the sick is not ascribed to the anointing with oil ...'. So why was I not healed? I was asked if I had the faith to believe this was possible and if I had unconfessed sin in my life. In the end I felt quite confused and after spending much time one night in fervent prayer based on the words, 'If ye have faith as a grain of mustard seed, ye shall say unto this mountain, remove hence', I questioned why the mountain of pain could not be removed from off my back? Did I really have faith to move mountains? Did I really believe God was able to effect healing? Indeed, was healing paramount? My thoughts ran amock, but I had no fresh inspiration. Of course I believed God was able to heal, when and as He chose, but He did not leave this ministry in the hands of man. What he did leave was an instruction to pray over the sick and an exhortation that prayer be accompanied by faith on the part of the sick person and on the part of the person praying. Prayer must be fervent but the raising up is always the Lord's prerogative.

While deeply appreciating the love and concern which motivated my dear friends I found myself growing weary of the subject. Why, should I want other than what God wanted for me? Why were Christians so pre-occupied with healing? I felt I could follow Spurgeon when he wrote, '... health is set before us as if it was the great thing to be desired above all other things. Is it so? I venture to say that the greatest earthly blessing that God can give to any of us is health, with the exception of sickness. Sickness has frequently been of more use to the saints of God than health has...'. Should I not, therefore, rest quietly in His will and pray for complete submission? I concluded that this is what God would have me to do and so I prayed according to His will for relief of pain, for direct healing by God Himself if He so chose, for grace to meet every new situation, for endurance to the end and for a willingness to work for Him with a broken body and a tired mind. At this time I had never heard of Peter Master's book, 'The Healing Epidemic', and I couldn't have argued with confidence my conviction that the gift of healing, like all the other gifts, were only for the early church, but within my being I felt this to be so. Unlike healing today, there were no failures in Christ's time. Reading this book clarified my thoughts and enhanced my understanding of the Apostolic gifts.

In the run up to London there were many issues requiring attention, but my priority had to be my radiotherapy treatment. I felt sad for my friends who were to accompany me on what should have been for all of us a very happy and exciting occasion. They felt so anxious for me and to make matters worse, I had my first experience of radiation sickness. I ended up going to London in a wheelchair but I did not find it demoralising. I was so thankful for any assistance which made life easier. Two days after I arrived in London I began to feel better. I was able to go to church on Sunday evening to what was a service of healing. As I observed those who went forward, I felt a tremendous joy welling up in my heart and I had a great urge to go up and share with those present what God can do in the absence of healing, for cancer and other diseases. This joy remained with me all evening. I felt as if the Lord was confirming that healing was not superior. His will was. I know I will be healed one day and I am content to await this wonderful moment, but it will not be on earth but in that place of which it is said, 'And there shall be no more death, neither sorrow nor crying, neither shall there be any more pain'. A body absent from all that corrupts and hampers here on earth. A body glorified.

But I am not absent from the body and I am conscious of all the impediments of a life lived out in a house of clay. I was very aware of this as I dressed for an occasion which I never expected to experience. Later, as I observed the Queen perform her duty I thought of the phrase, 'Weary lies the head that wears the crown'. But the overriding thoughts on this occasion were thoughts pertinent to eternity. Was our Sovereign Queen ready to meet her Sovereign King? The great leveller death gives the Monarch and her subject the same small portion of earth to hold their mortal remains, but this is not material, what is material is where death finds us and a lost eternity is an awful place to be in whether we live in a humble dwelling or in a rich and elaborate palace, but living in a palace seems to make a lost eternity even more awesome. I read of one who said, "Oh! that I had served my God as faithfully as I served my King, He would not then forsake my grey hairs" - it was the reign of King Edward VII. May the essence of this regret never be known to our Queen. How I longed to be able to speak with her about her soul. For weeks before this event I prayed for an opportunity to do so but this was denied and I felt disappointed. Seven seconds was accorded to each subject and not a second to spare. How difficult it is to find an opportunity to witness to the great. Their office prohibits it, but the Lord will find His own. As the last person left the palace, the gates were firmly closed. What thoughts this evoked. As we moved away sadness matched physical pain, but I felt thankful that the door of prayer remained open.

About nine days after I returned from London my hair fell out. I remember thinking before this happened that my long trusses had never seemed so beautiful. My hair had not been cut since, at the age of eighteen years, I started attending the prayer meeting. No one had said I should let it grow, although in those days it was unusual for a believer to have short hair. I just had a feeling it was the right thing to do. I used to think of the honour conferred on Mary when, with her crowning glory, she wiped the feet of her Saviour. And then I would think of the text, 'If a woman have long hair, it is a glory to her, for her hair is given her for a covering'. Biblical references, as much as anything, influenced me over the years and I felt that what was right for me at the outset of my Christian life should be right for me until the end. But now my long hair was gone. Surprisingly, I accepted it quite readily as in it I saw the hand of providence and as I did I knew that even if I were to live a number of years I would never again see my hair at the same length. This conclusion is based simply on the deduction that it will take about three months before any growth takes place and growth rate is then calculated at half to three quarters inch per month. Can I hope to arise at the resurrection with long hair? I know not, such a thought is but mere speculation. What I do know is that all things work together for good and while I do not enjoy wearing a wig His wisdom prevails. Luke's gospel outlines that 'the very hairs of our head are all numbered'. On this basis do I now lack a prerequisite? Not at all. God takes cognisance of every hair whether seen or unseen. Through this He is simply saying that He cares and watches over the minutest detail of our lives.

Chapter Nine

Friendship and Loneliness

❖

'Beareth all things, ... endureth all things'.
1st Cor. 13: 7

It may seem a strange combination to link these two
subjects together, but it makes a lot of sense to do so. Friendship is in many instances an antidote to loneliness and even to
aloneness, which while different from loneliness, often shares
the same dwelling. Many situations drive towards loneliness;
sickness, sorrow, loss, old age, singledom, to mention but a
few. It is unavoidable at some stage in our lives and although
the loneliness experienced by the believer can be placed in a
different category, nonetheless, it produces similar emotions.
In my own experience the single solitary state coupled with ill
health contributes to levels of loneliness hitherto unknown.
Not that this brings about covetous feelings at the happiness of
the married state, for neither state has any real value of itself,
in that neither is superior to the other. I'm sure there are many

who cannot agree with this, but the Lord raises the advantages and excellencies of both. Each separate star differs from another in glory. The state of the single life does have specific opportunities and its own blessedness but on the other hand it has depths of loneliness which none can comprehend except those who walk alone, humanly speaking. Loneliness brings its own suffering and it is to this trial that the joy of friendship acts as a great leavener. The life that is deprived of the affection of human love cannot communicate its own happiness to others and this accentuates the feelings of loneliness already prevalent. While I have known great depths of loneliness, especially in this last year as I find myself failing in bodily health, it is true to say that I have known the love of friends and the pervading sympathy which my infirmities awaken.

I don't know if I was ever more aware of the loneliness/ friendship affinity, if I can call it that, than when I was undertaking district nurse training. It brought home to me as a young nurse the extreme loneliness of old age when relatives and friends are long departed. This sad case should never be the experience of God's people, who as part of the body of believers should be loved for Christ's sake and yet, sadly, it is a very real problem faced by many elderly housed in our cities. They are in need of our prayers and our fellowship. This incident occurred in one of the poorer districts of a certain city. I was called to pay a first visit to an elderly lady living alone. I was given some sketchy details of the case as a consequence of which I arrived with a quantity of clothing. The door was open and as I entered I felt quite unprepared for the scene before my eyes. The dwelling, a room and kitchen, had the chill of many unfired Spring days. The general appearance was squalid, while the poor tenant, unable to meet the most basic requirements of hygiene and cleanliness was in a state of hypothermia, but she was still sufficiently in control to make it very clear that she did not want to leave her home. Why, with life ebbing away should she be so adamant? Because curled into her back, affording her the only warmth and comfort she knew was her Jack Russell terrier. Nothing but death would part her from him. A few hours later, with the house more inviting and a fire burning in the hearth, she was no more. The dying situation of this lonely old woman has remained etched in my memory these thirty four years. Who was she? What did she do in her working life? I know not, but she would have known family, she would have had friends and she would have earned her living as you and I do or did. Could it happen to us? In similar circumstances perhaps it could, but in obedience to God's command, 'Love thy neighbour as thy self', it ought not to. Is friendship necessary, is brotherly love essential? Very much so. Our mental, emotional and physical well being depends, to a great extent, upon it. We were not created to function independently of each other and we should thank our Lord for every manifestation of kindness shown towards us at each stage of living. Love is not an accident, it springs instinctively within our hearts and spurns us to fulfil the command, 'Love the brethren'. Members of Christ's body should find it impossible not to love their fellow members for love is the fulfilling of the law. Oh! the wonderful privileges which are ours as believers in the Lord Jesus Christ. Let us not abuse them but give them into His keeping.

Scripture clearly teaches that He who would have friends must show himself friendly, must delight in rendering service as well as bestowing good. It is like two embers which burn freely together or the knitting of heart to heart as described in the friendship between David and Jonathan, and expressed in David's impassioned song, 'I am distressed for thee my brother

Jonathan, very pleasant hast thou been to me. Thy love to me was wonderful'. Sometimes our departed friends mean more to us after they are taken away than when they were in our midst. We then realise the value of our friend by the void he or she leaves. True friendship does not diminish with time nor is it revoked by distance and silence does not produce awkwardness.

But the friendship of which I speak is rooted in the love of God. We are bonded to Christ by the unseen cord of His love to us 'Be ye kindly affectioned one to another with brotherly love, in honour preferring one another'. This is the friendship which influences for good, which bonds one to another with the bonds of self sacrifice and which we count among the dearest of all earthly gifts. In loneliness and the perplexities of life there is tremendous solace in the sincere affection of a single friend but when to this is added the fact that the heart is capable of differing degrees of friendship and of enjoying several friendships at the same time our hearts want to bless Him for His wonderful gifts. I once read that if friendship is of a high order, the soul of it is the worth of the one we call our friend. 'If the comparatively common and imperfect specimens of human nature can make impressions so delightful what must it have been to see closely that heart which was always beating with the purest love to God and man ... that character in which the minutest investigation has never detected a single spot or wrinkle'.

But friendships do not always run smoothly. Through familiarity we may cease to minister to our friends, cease to encourage them in the constancy of His love, cease to highlight our vast privileges, cease to remember that with all our imperfections we are His witnesses and cease to thank Him for the providence which brought us together in the first place. When this occurs, coldness and diminution of feeling results and gentleness is overtaken by actions and words which give rise to offence and friendship becomes stilted and painful. This should not be so in hallowed friendships and it cannot always be accounted for by acknowledging the frailties and sinfulness of our fallen human nature. A friend gladdens the heart, but when things go wrong this, sadly, is compensated by detachment and hurt. As Christians we should guard against infiltration by the enemy of souls. He does not want the Lord's people to dwell as friends in unity and immediately we feel the aching void of a marred relationship we should endeavour by His grace to submit our guilty heart to Him, seeking His restoration of our friendship. It is too precious to let it go and contrary to every command He gives us to love one another. I would be so much the poorer were it not for the bonds of loving friendships, cemented by the Lord who selects my every friend. Surely this kind of friendship is the dearest of earthly gifts bestowed by a loving Father who knows the ultimate needs of His children.

Little children love each other
Never give another pain
If your brother speaks in anger
Answer not in wrath again
Be not selfish to each other
Never mar another's rest
Strive to make another happy
And you will yourself be blest.

Chapter Ten

Whispers of Love

❖

'Come up hither'.
Rev. 11:12

Daughter,

Be of good cheer, it is I. You aren't toiling alone even although it seems like it. I am with you. I have seen your sadness and the heaviness of your heart. I know you are being buffeted at present, that you find it difficult to read or concentrate and that prayer, instead of being a joy, is a burden. You find your soul making no progress in holiness. Matters are so different from your expectation of the valley. But be of good cheer, you know I am a covenant keeping God and I will surely fulfil my promises.

I know how physically unwell you feel. I know the trauma through which you are passing. I know you cannot tell wither my favour is set upon you or not. I know you want assurances of my love. But is it not sufficient that I gave my Son, who is as great as Myself, for you. Nothing but love moved me to do this. I delight to give and to bless, the fountain of all grace is available to you. You are not going from weakness to weakness but from strength to strength. Did you not recently read that man is the chief of my works and that my children enjoy the most care of everything I have created. Pray for an increase in faith and in love. Remember no problem is isolated from me, no disappointment hid or insoluble. I know your concerns over lack of repentance, over sin, over lack of brokenness of heart. Jonathan Edwards audibly lamented his sins as he walked alone among the woods of New England. You have my ear, you can pour out your heart and bewail your sins as he did. You are presently sitting in darkness, can't you recall my promises, 'when I sit in darkness the Lord shall be a light unto me'. 'I am the light, in me is no darkness at all'.

I know the issues on your heart. You have prayed often about them and you have concluded that I do not hear. That there is no point in further praying about them. These are but the murmurings of Satan. Am I not known as the hearer of prayer? I answer in my way, in my time, but I always answer. Can't you recall that occasion when your cancer was confirmed, your bands of fear broken and you knew weeks of spiritual euphoria. You came to love your cancer simply because you experienced so much of my presence through it. Can I not do the same again, if through this you might grow in grace and in my knowledge? Stand still, my child, and know the salvation of your Lord.

Come poor sinner, chosen, accepted, redeemed, and view from afar off the dazzling splendour of the Mansion above where the beauty of holiness is seen at its exquisite best. Even with imperfect knowledge you can know something of the glory of eternity, of Paradise and the heaven of heavens. See the Master there as your Intercessor, see the adoring multitudes already within the veil, see the eternal throne, the centre and source of all joy and bliss and the innumerable company of angels who worship the Lord without ceasing. Observe the reverence with which the Lord, the great I Am, is worshipped. You will have no wandering thought there, no worldly affection or desire, nothing to mar your peace.

'And flesh and sin no more control
The sacred pleasures of the soul'.

The redeemed are happy there because they have been prepared and made partakers of holiness for, 'without holiness no man can see God'. Does this not whet your spiritual appetite and there is much, much more. No disease, sorrow or death, every tear wiped from their eyes by their God. A state where you will never cease to exist, where life will flow and flow and love will never grow cold. 'Before the mountains were brought forth or ever thou hadst formed the earth and the world, even from everlasting to everlasting thou art God'.

This life is entered by the redeemed at death. 'Whilst we are at home in the body we are absent from the Lord'. Immediate admission into the circle of the ransomed. No longer tired and listless but full of holy energy and activity, capable of enjoying God in a more perfect manner. How wonderful it will be to see the risen Lord in all His glorified humanity. As one of the divines wrote, 'The humanity of the Lord will be the tabernacle in which the glory of His divinity will reside, and through which its splendour will shine forth, with a brightness which will fill heaven with unspeakable joy'.

The Lord is very close to his dying saints and sends an innumerable company of angels to minister unto His heirs of salvation and to accompany their souls into life everlasting. Not one soul for whom He died lost. Clad in the white celestial robes given unto each one of them, they ascend, 'a great multitude which no man can number, of every kindred and tongue and nation to stand before the throne'. Conquerers through Him that loved them and gave Himself for them, they wave their palms of victory and cry with a loud voice, 'salvation to our God which sitteth upon the Throne, and unto the Lamb'. In this life of glory where everything is calculated to secure and increase the happiness of the redeemed they will inherit the white stone with their immortal name engraven upon it, and they will serve Him day and night in His temple, every moment opening endless sources of pleasure and happiness before them. As one of old wrote, 'They shall make an eternal progression into the fulness of God'. Their glorified resurrected bodies enjoying a state of perfected ecstasy and all that was sealed up in mystery while on earth now discernible. Soul, do you not long to be there, to sing in sweet melody the refrain of Heaven? No one out of tune and no one without a song. The eyes of the blind and the ears of the deaf opened and for the first time the tongue of the dumb singing.

In the words of the hymn writer, can they not exclaim,

'And is this heaven, and am I here
How short the road, how swift the flight,
I am all life, all eye, all ear
Jesus is here, my soul's delight'.

Having brought this theme thus far I find my thoughts totally inadequate. I cannot portray the heights of this blessed state nor can I proclaim the ineffable glory of heaven. And how can I, mere human that I am, when, 'eye hath not seen, nor ear heard, neither have entered into the heart of man the things which God hath prepared for them that love Him'. Reader, discern the glories of this City by studying the Word of God. Get to know the treasures of your Home by frequent meditation on the infallible Truth. Such meditation is most sweet.

'Whatsoever things are true, whatsoever things are honest, whatsoever things are just, whatsoever things are pure, whatsoever things are lovely, whatsoever things are of good report, if there be any virtue, and if there be any praise, think on these things'.

Epilogue

❖

'Let the whole earth be filled with His glory.'
Psa. 72:19

Throughout the writing of this book I have at times felt quite unwell. As a result I have required to leave out at least two chapters and to shorten others. As I re-read it I cannot but feel an inadequacy of thought and presentation, but nevertheless I hope it will convey to the reader one woman's journey with cancer and God's provision to meet her need.

Recently a local school asked a class of twelve year old pupils to write a speech on, 'The bravest person I know'. I was overwhelmed to learn that one pupil, not well known to me, chose me as her subject. I do not count myself brave, I have done nothing outstanding which would place me in this category. Like thousands of other sufferers I have walked a path mapped out for me and I have responded to each stage through God's sustaining grace.

As the reader works through this account it will be obvious that there is progression of disease, but through every painful meander the application of God's grace is sure. It is those who overcome who will receive a white stone with a new name written on it. My constant prayer is, 'Help me Lord to overcome and prepare me for eternity'.

I can find no better way to sum up than in the words of Richard Baxter, who used to say, "Press on, Richard, to the saints everlasting rest". To myself, I say, press on.